7 WAYS TO STAY

RESTED

for lazy reader

by

MARGIE MAE

7 Ways To Stay Rested

for lazy reader

Margie Mae

7Ways to Stay Rested

First Edition

The publication of this book is a symbol of strenght from someone who push through life. Its a small sign of victory for the author who have all the reason to quit, yet choose to give life. From the chaos and surprises of life and from what felt like loosing a dream to finding hope and peace in the hidden intelligence of rest.

I acknowlegde that experiencing peace in my case is not possible without the help of higher power i call Yeshua, thank you God, for the divine help and invisible guidance.

To my friend Danne, who listen to every dream I have and carry it to heaven, you remind me how short and precious life is. Thank you.

To my close friends and family, my strenght and support. thank you.

To my readers whos seeking to increase the presence of peace in their lives. Thank you for choosing this! together were going after a worth seeking gem. -
PEACE and Rest

-MM

It's a CHOICE

To stay rested is a CHOICE. If you genuinely cherish this, you must consciously opt, day after day, perhaps even multiple times daily, to vigilantly preserve your serenity and protect your PEACE. What does this entail? It's akin to safeguarding the sanctity of your heart and the purity of your thoughts. Your heart and mind are precious assets, entrusted to your care, a very precious possesion and it is solely your duty to guard, to nurture and to shield them

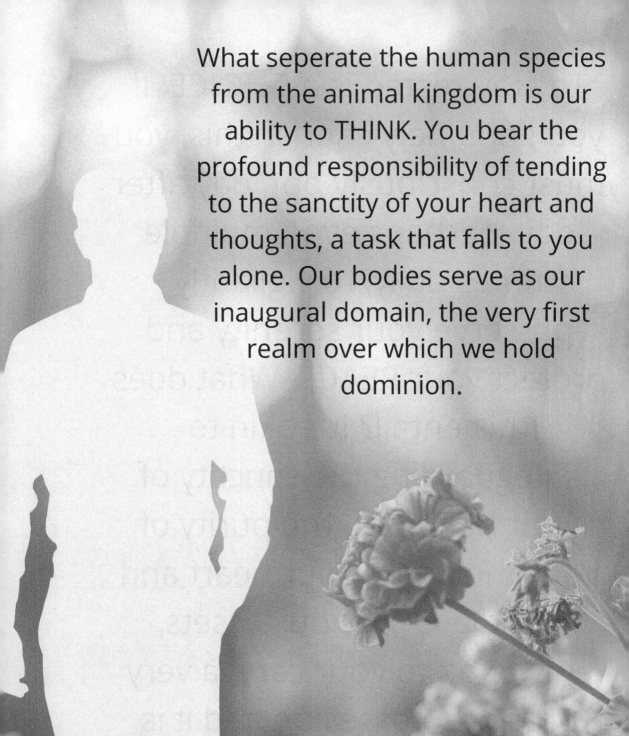

What seperate the human species from the animal kingdom is our ability to THINK. You bear the profound responsibility of tending to the sanctity of your heart and thoughts, a task that falls to you alone. Our bodies serve as our inaugural domain, the very first realm over which we hold dominion.

Restful and peaceful people abstain from attributing responsibility to others or their surroundings. They understand that the onus lies solely upon them for regulating what enters and exits their sphere of influence. The energy they project and permit into their lives is contingent upon their own discernment, self impose bounderies and self-empowerment. Such is their remarkable potency. Your POWERFUL!!!

Individuals committed to inner peace make a conscious effort to avoid nurturing bitterness, anger, malice, hatred, or any negative energy within themselves. They prioritize the well-being of their thoughts and emotions, fostering a positive and harmonious inner landscape.

Practice with me:

I say...

"As an intentional act of my will, I choose to release fear, depression, bitterness uncertainty and unforgiveness—both towards myself and others. I cast aside hopelessness and anxiety, promptly and securely uninstalling them from my being—right now!
Furthermore, I choose to replace and install peace, joy, light, love, healing, and wisdom, accepting these gifts wholeheartedly—here and now!"

This will be an ongoing endeavor until it becomes second nature. I have often found myself repeating this affirmation multiple times throughout the day, especially during the initial stages when I began instructing my body to walk in the paths of light and serenity.

.

Our bodies tend to gravitate toward the environment in which we were nurtured and the memories of the past. Nevertheless, retraining oneself to stride confidently into the future's vision, walking in peace and tranquility, is a precious pursuit indeed.

For Christians allowing the Prince of Peace to search our inner being and giving him a permission to work in us and thru us is also ways to cultivate peace. It gives that sense of calmness more than the human mind can understand nor comprehend. Everyone has different beliefs, choose what works for you best.

Be Grateful

GRATE
FUL

Nurture a spirit of gratitude.

Individuals who find inner peace possess a remarkable ability to uncover the silver linings in every circumstance. They consistently cultivate a sense of gratitude in all aspects of their lives. When it comes to relationships, they trade lofty expectations for genuine appreciation. With unwavering childlike faith, they discern treasures and opportunities in every situation. They recognize that gratitude isn't just a mindset; it's a powerful multiplier that enhances their well-being and the well-being of those around them

THEY REPLACE

Their

With

EXPECTATION

thank
y♥u

APPRECIATION

They consistently nurture a mindset of gratitude, elevating their vibrational frequency. They cultivate a vibrant garden of thoughts, understanding that gratitude fosters happiness, rewires their brain, enhances self-esteem, strengthens their immune system, and alleviates stress. They recognize that a grateful heart acts as a magnetic force for attracting miracles.

A GREATFUL HEART

is a marget for

MIRACLES

Affirmation:

I am so happy and grateful for the fact that my body is now in harmony with my goals. Im so grateful for the strength and health and I celebrate my intuition and brilliance, choosing to embrace the path it was uniquely created for me.
I am happy and grateful that my circumstances are alligning and working for my good and the people around me.
I am filled with happiness and gratitude, now that i have everything i need to succeed and win to achieved my goals and make this my reality.

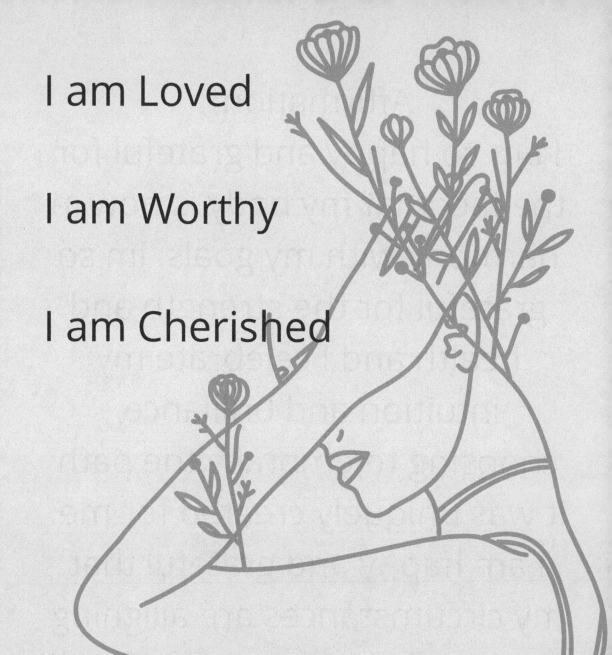

I am Loved

I am Worthy

I am Cherished

I am victorious and I'm winning. It feels good working my BEST.

I am grateful that Love, Joy, Romance, flow easily into my life

I
LOVE
WHO I
AM
BECO
MING

Be
Authentic

"People who have attained a state of inner peace and tranquility are at ease with their imperfections, and they possess a keen awareness of their strengths and weaknesses. They understand the universal truth that nobody has everything neatly sorted out.

They acknowledge that it's perfectly normal not to feel okay sometimes. However, their distinction lies in their adeptness at communicating their needs, desires, and thoughts in a respectful and constructive manner. Rather than reacting impulsively with anger, they respond with love and a willingness to forgive.

In their world, prioritizing LOVE and connection takes precedence over the need to prove themselves right."

They communicate with gentleness because their inner confidence radiates from within. They do not rely on external approval to find happiness; instead, they have found peace within themselves.

Indeed, authenticity derives from aligning with your genuine self, adhering to the core essence of WHO you are. You were created to give and receive and for LOVE, inherently deserving of it. Embracing your status as a masterpiece, recognizing your inherent worth, and acknowledging your potential for greatness in the present moment is the true treasure. Remaining connected to what ignites your passion is the essence of staying authentic to yourself.

Finding and
acknowledging
what sparks
you is staying
true to yourself.

Embracing the art of receiving help and graciously sharing with others is staying authentic to yourself

We are beautifully crafted to operate as a collective, as a community, each of us with a unique role to play. Discovering your niche, finding your purpose, seeking wisdom, and accepting love and support from others is a profound part of self-discovery. When we unite, we achieve more, and the magic of teamwork turns dreams into reality. TEAM WORKS MAKES THE DREAM WORKS.

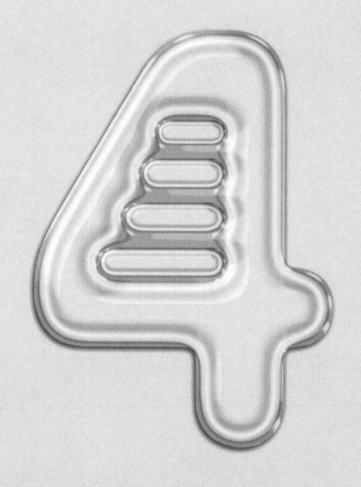

Change your Evironment

Transform Your Surroundings with Love: Let's explore the beautiful art of creating a space that truly reflects your heart's desires. Peaceful souls, those who cherish tranquility, also cherish their personal havens. They carefully choose what brings them joy, letting go of things that burden their spirits. Hoarding is not their way; they embrace simplicity. They treat their space with deep respect and lovingly craft an environment that radiates restfulness, authenticity, and utmost comfort, aligning perfectly with their unique selves.

their living spaces function in harmony with them, rather than requiring them to adapt constantly. Weekends are not consumed by endless cleaning tasks because they've learned gentle art of keeping things organized throughout the week. Their approach is one of love and intention, ensuring that their space not only reflects their identity but also provides them with the comfort and support they deserve.

They wholeheartedly recognize that their space is a precious extension of themselves, and they've thoughtfully established boundaries to nurture it. Every corner is a testament to their unique taste, intentionally designed to evoke a sense of inner peace and serenity.

Focus on your Vision

If you wake up every morning and your not defined by a vision of your future, then your left with the memories of the past and your life will be predictable. -Dr. Joe Dispeza

Restful people purposefully shape their future. They refrain from dwelling on their past, avoiding the unnecessary rekindling of emotions rooted in pain and uncertainty. They choose not to persist in misery, recognizing that they can consciously guide their body, affirming the mastery of their mind. Each day, they make a conscious decision to shift their thought patterns towards positivity and growth they are aware that its going to be uncomfortable but they are committed to their vision. Its their vision that keeps them alive. Its their vision that gives them purpose to live.

Lazer

What you focus on

Focus

Your

Choice

By empowering yourself to now accept and trust your ability to choose your focus daily and your capacity to direct and focus your attention in any direction you choose, you will recognize and now accept the power within you to focus and pay attention each and every day in the achievement of your goals and dreams.

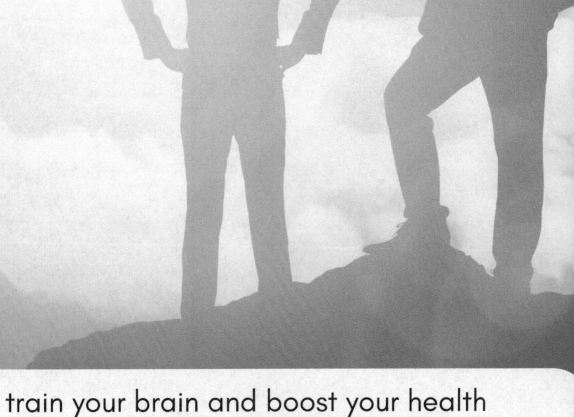

train your brain and boost your health
Visit: https://iRest.World

You can also choose right now and be aware and release any disempowering thoughts, emotions or behavior that cause you to be unfocus and scattered in your efforts. Choose to move away from and release any disempowering habits that doesnt serve your greatest good and success.

as each day and night passes you will also notice how much easier it is to see, feel and enjoy the process and the positive results from now on.

Forgive

Develop a

A lifestyle of forgiveness.

Practice with me:

I say...

As an act of my will, i choose to forgive you _____, I release you and you owe me nothing! Thank you for the experience that shape me to be stronger and more resilient me. Thank you for helping me identify what i don't want in life. I release you NOW. I choose peace, Im forgiving you to free myself from any hurt and disappointment now and ever. And as an act of my will i choose to bless you. Not just to blessed you but to really blessed you.

Sometimes the hardest people to forgive is yourself but you need to release yourself from every form of hatred, disappointment, expectations and learn to be kind and compassionate to yourself because its the person you deal every minute, you go to bed with it and you wake up with it. Its been with you as long as you live and you find more peace in life if your at peace with yourself. And when your generous to forgive self, you'll find it easier to give forgiveness others.

FORGIVENESS LETTER TO SELF

Dear [Your Name],
I am writing this letter to you, to the most important person in my life, with a heart full of compassion and understanding. It is time for forgiveness, self-forgiveness and let go of the past.
Over the years, I have carried the weight of my mistakes, regrets, and the pain I caused myself. I have held onto guilt, shame, and self-criticism, as if they were my constant companions. I have berated myself for my imperfections and judged myself harshly for the choices I've made.
Today, I want to release that burden and offer myself the forgiveness and love that I deserve.
I forgive myself for all the times I made mistakes, big or small. Mistakes are opportunities for growth and learning.
I forgive myself for the times I doubted my worth and value. I am inherently valuable and deserving of love and kindness.
I forgive myself for any past hurtful or negative self-talk. I recognize that I am not defined by my thoughts, and I have the power to change them. I want you to know, dear self, that you are worthy of love, forgiveness, and happiness. You are deserving of all the good things that life has to offer. From this moment forward, I promise to treat myself with kindness, compassion, and acceptance.

With Love and Forgiveness,
(Your Name)

Restful and peaceful people undersrtand that lifestyle of forgiveness is part of the process of becoming.

they delight in giving mercy

they know that deep inside it will always comes back to them.

for christians they believe the ancient book of Matthew that state: blessed are the merciful for they will obtain mercy.

to the person you want

BECOME

WHATEVER IS TRUE,
WHATEVER IS PURE
WHATEVER IS LOVELY
IF ANYTHING IS EXCELLENT OR
PRAISEWORTHY

THINK ABOUT
SUCH THING

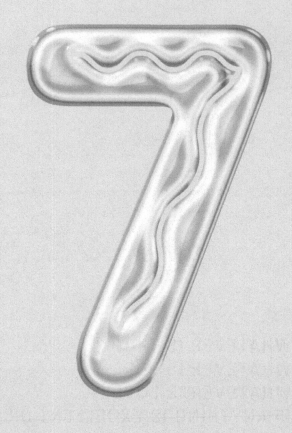

Meditate

When you have an idea, you think it in your brain, linger on that idea , meditate on it and and F E E L it in your heart

There....

conception is taking place.

As the old saying say,

What you seek is inside of you

Have you ever thought what it is like to have a peaceful life? What it is like to be a winner? What it is like to have courage, to be wealthy, to be happy? What it is like to experience bliss and harmony?

What does that look like to you?

I'm going to ask you to STOP
reading and imagine that life ...

Now, put your emotion into it. Imagine that your living that

NOW

What do you see?

What do you smell?

What does it taste like?

What did you feel?

(did you salivate seeing the lemon? this is how important visualization is, your body can't distinguish what is true and what is imagined) are you able to hold that thought for 7 secs? How about try for 14secs? are you able to hold that for 5 mins? Lets try 7 mins next time.

You get the idea.

its not an intellectual process its a heartfelt feeling process and allow yourself to embrace this emotion and pictures. If you do this over and over your body will to be lifted to a new mind.

do this over and over again and your installing a software.

that software in time it becomes a hardware and it become your personality

the next thing you know it your already acting a more peaceful person.

The HeartMath Institute dedicate more than 25 years of research focus on physiology of the mind and body coherence.
The way our brain works, humans naturally doesn't like change speciallyunexpected ones, as it turn out one of the most effective way to relieve anxiety or feeling overwhelmed is to access the intelligence of the heart and shift that rhytm of the heart which send a different neurometric to the brain,. to help you make a better choices in the moment and help you really navigate this stressful times.

Interestingly a lot of people surprise to know that the heart sends more information to the nervouse system, to the brain than the other way around
This sound like a new discovery but its not, its been known since the late 1800.

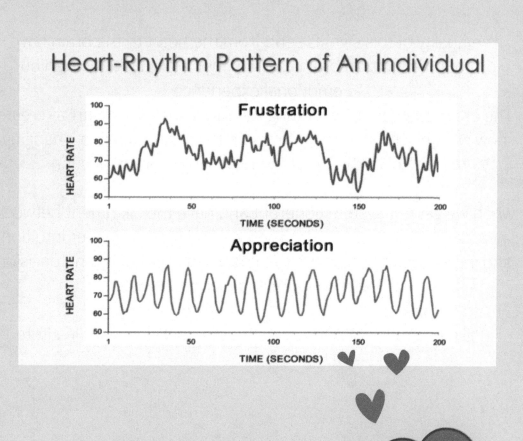

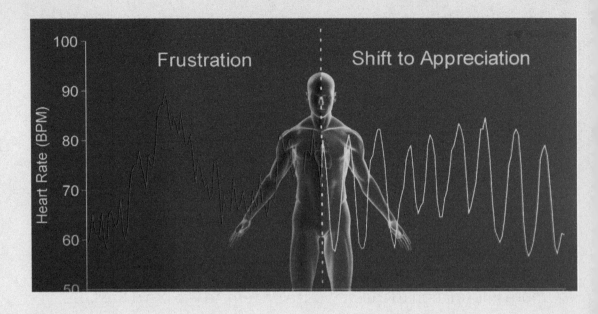

The quality of this signals send from the heart to the brain have profound effects on brain function, our mental clarity even our emotional experience
The brain is largely interpretting the signal from the heart to create how we feel. This is why we focus on the heart so much, changing the rhtytm of the heart, clearly improve brain function.

when we get our system coherent and have the alignment between heart and brain, thats really when we access that deeper intuition and inner guidance, so we have a new sense of clarity and decision what may seem complex otherwise.

-Rollin McCraty, PhD DIrector of Research, HeartMath Institute

When your mind,

your heart

your words

and your hand

are in Alignment

things flows

Guided Meditation: GENERAL

Cultivating Inner Peace

1. **Settle In (1-2 minutes):** Find a comfortable position, close your eyes, and take a few deep breaths. Inhale deeply through your nose, and exhale slowly through your mouth. Let go of any tension in your body.
2. **Body Scan (2 minutes):** Bring your awareness to your toes. Notice any sensations there, and then gradually move your focus up through your feet, ankles, calves, and so on, all the way up to the top of your head. Let go of any tension as you go.
3. **Center in the Heart (1-2 minutes):** Shift your attention to the center of your chest, where your heart resides. Visualize a warm, radiant light in this area. This is your heart's center, your source of love and compassion.
4. **Heart Breathing (2-3 minutes):** Begin to breathe slowly and deeply in and out through your heart center. As you inhale, imagine a gentle, calming light entering your heart. With each exhale, release any stress or negativity. Continue this heart-focused breathing.
5. **Positive Emotion (2-3 minutes):** Bring to mind a moment of deep joy, love, or gratitude. Visualize this moment in detail, reliving the positive emotions it brought you. Let those feelings expand in your heart.

Guided Meditation: GENERAL

Cultivating Inner Peace

6. **Radiate Love (2 minutes):** Now, envision sending this love and positivity out into the world. Visualize it as a radiant light extending from your heart, enveloping your loved ones, and expanding further to embrace all living beings. Feel the interconnectedness of all.

7. **Intention Setting (2-3 minutes):** Take a moment to set a personal intention or affirmation. What positive change or growth would you like to cultivate in your life? Formulate a clear and concise intention, and repeat it silently to yourself.

8. **Gratitude (1-2 minutes):** Express gratitude for this time you've devoted to yourself and your inner peace. Be thankful for the love and positivity you've cultivated within.

9. **Closing (1-2 minutes):** Slowly return your awareness to your physical surroundings. Wiggle your fingers and toes, gently open your eyes, and come back to the present moment. Carry this sense of inner peace and positivity with you throughout your day.

Remember, this is a practice, and it's perfectly normal for your mind to wander. Each time you notice it has strayed, gently guide it back to the meditation. Regular practice can help you find greater peace, reduce stress, and nurture your inner well-being. Thank you for joining me in this meditation session.

Guided Meditation: Scripture base

Cultivating Inner Peace with Scripture

1. **Settle In (1-2 minutes)**: Find a comfortable, quiet place to sit or lie down. Close your eyes gently, and take a few deep breaths. Inhale deeply through your nose, and exhale slowly through your mouth. As you do, remember the words of Psalm 46:10, "Be still, and know that I am God."

2. **Body Scan (2 minutes):** Begin by grounding yourself. Imagine roots extending from your body into the Earth, connecting you to God's creation. Let go of any tension, remembering the words from Matthew 11:28, "Come to me, all who labor and are heavy laden, and I will give you rest."

3. **Center in the Heart (1-2 minutes)**: Shift your attention to the center of your chest, where your heart resides. Visualize a warm, radiant light in this area. This is your heart's center, a place of divine love.

4. **Heart Breathing (2-3 minutes):** Breathe slowly and deeply in and out through your heart center. As you inhale, imagine God's love and peace filling your heart. With each exhale, release any stress or negativity. Reflect on the words from Philippians 4:7, "And the peace of God, which surpasses all understanding, will guard your hearts and your minds in Christ Jesus."

5. **Positive Emotion (2-3 minutes):** Bring to mind a moment of deep gratitude or love, as inspired by Colossians 3:15: "And let the peace of Christ rule in your hearts, to which indeed you were called in one body. And be thankful." Feel these emotions expanding in your heart.

Note: Your reading scripture base sample, there is a general sample in the previous page.

Guided Meditation: Scripture base

Cultivating Inner Peace with Scripture

6. **Radiate Love (2 minutes):** Visualize God's love flowing from your heart as a radiant light, embracing your loved ones and extending further to all living beings, echoing the words of John 13:34, "A new command I give you: Love one another. As I have loved you, so you must love one another."

7. **Intention Setting (2-3 minutes):** Set a personal intention or affirmation inspired by Philippians 4:13: "I can do all things through him who strengthens me." What positive change or growth would you like to cultivate in your life? Formulate a clear intention, and repeat it silently to yourself.

8. **Gratitude (1-2 minutes):** Express gratitude for this sacred time you've devoted to yourself and your inner peace. Thank God for the love and positivity you've cultivated within.

9. **Closing (1-2 minutes):** Slowly return your awareness to your physical surroundings. Wiggle your fingers and toes, gently open your eyes, and come back to the present moment. Carry this sense of inner peace, divine love, and God's presence with you throughout your day.

Thank you for joining me in this meditation session. If you want to have more of meditation scripture go to
www.iREST.WORLD

Give

BONUS PAGE

Do not wait for your healing to take place, give anyway

You never know what will come back to you when you give wholeheartedly and with joy

Anyway
Poem by Mother Teresa

People are often unreasonable, illogical and self centered;
Forgive them anyway.

If you are kind, people may accuse you of selfish, ulterior
motives;
Be kind anyway.

If you are successful, you will win some false friends and some
true enemies;
Succeed anyway.

If you are honest and frank, people may cheat you;
Be honest and frank anyway.

What you spend years building, someone could destroy
overnight;
Build anyway.

If you find serenity and happiness, they may be jealous;
Be happy anyway.

The good you do today, people will often forget tomorrow;
Do good anyway.

Give the world the best you have, and it may never be enough;
Give the world the best you've got anyway.

You see, in the final analysis, it is between you and your God;
It was never between you and them anyway.

Whatever you sow you will reap.

This is true both the positive
and the negative. If you sow
hatred, you'll reap hatred, if
you sow unforgivenes, you'll
reap unforgivenes, if you sow
mercy you'll reap mercy, if you
sow peace you'll reap peace. If
you sow love you'll reap love.
If you sow sparingly, you'll
reap sparingly. If you sow
generously youl reap
generously.

Its a universal law, it's not a man made law. No one is excempted. Everything will come back in it's time.

In the time of uncertainty, chaos and fear...

RESTFUL PEOPLE

Choose to eminate

FREE DOWNLOAD

5 Easy Steps to Boost
Your Income and
Relaxation

Build Unstoppable Confidence
to Manifest Abundance in 2023,
Paving the Way for an
Empowered 2024!

Visit Us :
https:iRest.world

BE YOU
DREAM
BIG

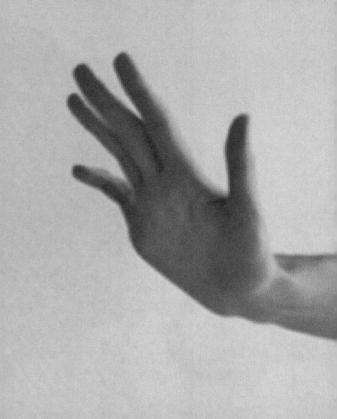

https://www.lifewave.com/irest

https://iRest.world

Margie Mae

Are you in need of Rejuvenation but dont know where to start? Have you been labeled as 'lazy' when deep down you know that it's not about laziness, but a longing for motivation and a clearer vision? "7 ways to stay Rested" is a simple easy to read, start-up guide, your gentle, loving companion, to rekindling your motivation and purpose.

In "7 Ways to Stay Rested," we reveal a path to revitalization that's perfect for those who know that true success isn't about hustling harder but finding what fuels you inside.

It's time to take this loving journey and revitalize your life.

iRest